LEOPARDS AND CHEETAHS

BY MARIE PEARSON

Published by The Child's World®
1980 Lookout Drive • Mankato, MN 56003-1705
800-599-READ • www.childsworld.com

Photographs ©: Light Stock/iStockphoto, cover (leopard), 2, 8, 20, 24 (leopard); Stuart G. Porter/ Shutterstock Images, cover (cheetah), 2–3, 14, 16, 21, 24 (cheetah); Chaithanya Krishnan/Shutterstock Images, 5; Ondrej Chvatal/Shutterstock Images, 6; Ben Landy/iStockphoto, 9; Andre Marais/ Shutterstock Images, 10; Ben Landy/Shutterstock Images, 13; Eugen Haag/Shutterstock Images, 17; iStockphoto, 19

ISBN 9781503835924
LCCN 2019943062

Printed in the United States of America

ABOUT THE AUTHOR

Marie Pearson is a children's book author and editor. She especially loves learning about animals and nature.

TABLE OF CONTENTS

CHAPTER 1

Spotted Cats

A large cat **stalks** through Kenya's grasslands. Its fur is tan with black spots. Two round ears prick up at a distant sound. The large cat's teeth are sharp. Is it a cheetah or a leopard? How are they different?

Cheetahs call Africa home.

Leopards have both solid spots and rosettes.

CHAPTER 2

Leopards

Leopards have short, tan fur with a lighter belly. They have some solid black spots. They also have rosettes. These round shapes have black outlines with tan in the middle.

Leopards have long bodies with short legs. They are **stocky**. They are 20 to 30 inches (60 to 70 cm) at the shoulder. They weigh 110 to 200 pounds (50 to 90 kg). Their claws fully **retract**.

Leopards are found all over Africa and Asia, in grasslands, deserts, and even rain forests!

Leopards are powerful enough to pull entire gazelles into trees to eat.

The cats wait for **prey** to come close. Then they **pounce**. Leopards are powerful. They can catch prey ten times heavier than themselves. They drag their food into a tree to eat. Leopards eat many things. Their prey includes **gazelles** and wild pigs.

Leopards can purr and growl. They also roar.

CHAPTER

3

Cheetahs

Cheetahs have short, tan fur. The color is lighter on their bellies. Their bodies are covered in solid black spots. A black stripe runs from the inner corners of their eyes and down the sides of their **muzzles**. This stripe is called a tear mark.

Cheetahs have black tear marks on their faces.

Cheetahs use their tails to help make quick turns while hunting.

Cheetahs are tall and **lean**. They are built for speed. They are about 30 inches (77 cm) at the shoulder. They can weigh 75 to 140 pounds (34 to 64 kg). The cats can run 70 miles per hour (112 km/h). This speed helps them catch prey. They mainly eat gazelles. Cheetahs sometimes eat smaller mammals, too.

Cheetahs' claws cannot retract all the way. The claws dig into the ground as the cats run. They only rarely climb trees.

Cheetahs can purr. They growl, hiss, and make many other sounds, too. They do not roar.

Cheetahs live and hunt in grasslands, deserts, and dry forests across Africa.

CHAPTER

4

What's the Difference?

Leopards have some solid spots and rosettes. Cheetahs have solid spots. Leopards do not have tear marks. Cheetahs do. Leopards are powerful. Cheetahs are fast. Leopards can roar. But cheetahs can't.

Leopards are part of the big cat family, which includes lions, tigers, and jaguars. Cheetahs are not because they cannot roar.

These cats are very different. But they are the same in some ways. Both have round ears. They can purr. And both are perfect at what they do!

LEOPARDS

- Weigh 110 to 200 pounds (50 to 90 kg)
- Powerful climbers
- Can roar

CHEETAHS

- Weigh 75 to 140 pounds (34 to 64 kg)
- Fast runners
- Do not roar

GLOSSARY

gazelles (guh-ZELS) Gazelles are deer-like antelopes with a pair of horns. Cheetahs and leopards hunt gazelles.

lean (LEEN) Something that is lean is thin. Cheetahs are lean.

muzzles (MUZZ-elz) Muzzles are the noses and mouths of animals. Cheetahs have tear marks next to their muzzles.

pounce (POWNSS) To pounce is to leap suddenly onto something. Leopards pounce on their prey.

prey (PRAY) Prey are animals that are eaten by other animals. Gazelles are common prey for cheetahs and leopards.

retract (ree-TRAKT) Something that can retract can be drawn in. Leopard claws can retract into a special part of their paws.

stalks (STAHKS) An animal that stalks walks slowly and watchfully. A leopard stalks its prey.

stocky (STAH-kee) Something that is stocky is thick. Leopards are stocky.

TO LEARN MORE

IN THE LIBRARY

Bishop, Nic. *Big Cats*. New York, NY: Scholastic, 2019.

Simon, Seymour. *Big Cats*. New York, NY: Harper, 2017.

Waldendorf, Kurt. *How Fast Is a Cheetah?* Mankato, MN: The Child's World, 2017.

ON THE WEB

Visit our website for links about leopards and cheetahs:
childsworld.com/links

Note to Parents, Teachers, and Librarians: We routinely verify our Web links to make sure they are safe and active sites. So encourage your readers to check them out!

ACTIVITY

Draw a picture of a leopard and a cheetah. Your picture should clearly show the differences between the leopard and the cheetah. Look at pages 20 and 21 for help.

INDEX